C000259880

SWANSEA
Memories
are made of this!

by David Roberts

Published by Bryngold Books Ltd
100 Brynau Wood, Cimla,
Neath, South Wales SA11 3YQ.

Typesetting, layout, editing and
design by Bryngold Books
Copyright © Bryngold Books 2015.

ISBN 978-1-905900-39-8

All rights reserved. No part of this publication may be reproduced, stored in a retrieval system, or
transmitted in any form, or by any means, electronic, mechanical, photocopying, recording, or otherwise
without the prior permission, in writing, of the copyright holder, nor be otherwise circulated in any form
or binding or cover other than that in which it is published and without a similar condition being
imposed on the subsequent publisher.

www.bryngoldbooks.com

About the author

When David Roberts set out to gather material for a pictorial nostalgia book on Swansea little did he realise that so successful would that first publication be it would signal the start of a long running series. **Swansea — *Memories are made of this***, is the 18th book he has collated in as many years, something which is no mean achievement.

David Roberts

In that time he has drawn together many thousands of images each one of which is an important piece in the fascinating jigsaw that is Swansea's past. The enduring series is now a part of the city's calendar and its annual arrival eagerly awaited. Nowhere else can claim such a continually growing, easily accessible guide to the way life once was in the community, but perhaps more importantly one to which everyone in the community can contribute. A former journalist, David has witnessed first hand many of the changes that feature in his books and is proud to play a part in making sure we never forget our roots.

The Mumbles lifeboat, William Gammon, and its crew at sea in Swansea Bay during the early 1970s. The vessel was in service at the station from 1947 until 1974.

A big thank you

Swansea — Memories are made of this! is a book that has only been made possible with the help and encouragement of many people, not least all those who have shared and allowed the use of their fantastic photographs of people, places and events.

These contributions, both large and small capture times from the city's past and allow it to be seen from a different perspective, often through the eyes of those who were there, camera in hand. We are grateful for the involvement of: The South Wales Evening Post, Bryn Willcock, Raymond & Dorothy Lewis, Robin Wayne, Hazel Rees, John Southard, Bernard Humphries, Hilary Evans, Sandra Hayden, David Govier, Alan Williams, Colin Andrew, Steve Davies, Jean Evans, Robert Davies, Robert Wayne Davies, Julie Jones, J.V. Hughes, Steve Phillips, Roy Kneath, John Wilks, Geoff Rees, Paul Smith, Clive Cockings, Colin Riddle, Keith Roberts, Hugh Rees, Roger Evans, Dr J. Adrian Williams, Des Jeffreys, John Roberts, Adeline Evans, Roger Green, Richard & Anne Evans, Mike Hallett, Bill Morris, Rita Lewis, Tony Barrett, Christine Lewis, Terry Beynon, Wendie John, Vivian G. Davies, Sylvia & Bernard Miles, Irene Willis, John Jones, Peter Muxworthy, Louise Watkins, Ken & Marie John, Eric Hill, Graham Davies, Peter Nedin, Chris Taylor, Barry Jones, Kathryn Owens, Roger Fordham, Angela Gowman, Jennifer Pember, John Murphy, Stephen Miles, Hywel B. Weaver, Bill Lumber, Miss D. W. Powell, Roy Morgan, John Hughes, Christine Rix, Bryndon Evans, Maisie Hayman, Charlotte Barry, William Bateman, Eddie Ford, Andrew Jones, Charlie Wise, Katherine Rapsey, Christopher Matthews, Norman Hurford & Peter Brabham.

Others without whose help the book would not have appeared include Charlie Wise, Neil Melbourne and David Beynon. Finally, I must, as ever, thank my wife Cheryl for her unfailing support. Without that I am sure the task would have been far more difficult to achieve.

Your pictures count

If you have photographs of people, places or events in and around Swansea right up to recent times then you could play a part in the next Swansea nostalgia book. Please telephone 01639 643961 or e-mail david.roberts@bryngoldbooks.com to discover the ways in which you can do this. Only the involvement of people like yourself keeps this intriguing record alive. All photographs, transparencies, negatives, black and white or colour, of people, places, events, streets, buildings, schooldays and sport are considered whatever their age, subject or format. They are all promptly returned. We can also receive your pictures electronically. Meanwhile, if you have missed any of the previous 17 books then contact us now as some titles are still available to help complete your collection. You can also check out our many other titles at
www.bryngoldbooks.com

Keeping the memory alive

Swansea, as those familiar with the proud city will testify, is constantly evolving, rarely pausing for breath in its quest to keep up. As a result its citizens find themselves enduring an ever changing way of life. The pace of such change can often be bullet-like. Facets of the way this historic waterside metropolis once appeared can vanish without trace and like its places, 21st Century Swansea's people, their faces and fashions, also come and go.

While the memory will keep alive images of major city landmarks it can often dim when less recognised subjects are brought to mind. Sometimes only the random click of a camera shutter will have captured a subject missed by most. Such photographs may have been hidden away in cherished family albums, but there is no doubt that they have a useful part to play in charting the continual development of the community that is Swansea.

Looking back at the way things once were can evoke feelings of nostalgia or moisten the eye, but some photographs in this book, gathered from many different sources, may also raise an eyebrow at just how significantly change has imposed itself on this glorious seaside city.
Some images reveal that where once there was nothing now there stand markers for the future or conversely where once a familiar building stood now there is simply emptiness.
The people who fill its streets and suburbs; its schools and shopping centres are important too and those featured within will each have played their part in the social history of this bold and innovative hub.

There will be few unable to identify with some aspect of the record of the city that
Swansea — Memories are made of this! offers. The pictures are likely to unleash a myriad of emotion, but they all contribute greatly to the recording of everyday life in a city determined to stay at the forefront in the 21st Century march for progress.

David Roberts, 2015.

When the sun shines and the temperatures rise everyone heads for the bays! It seems that was exactly the case when this sunny afternoon scene was snapped at Caswell Bay, during the summer of 1984.

Scouts and leaders of the 20th Swansea, 1st Morriston (Clase) Scouts during their Canadian tour, 1996.

Members of Swansea Dolphins Swimming Club at a fundraising stall at a Singleton Park event, 1990.

An energetic paper boy at Fforestfach leaps a gate at Llwyn Derw to deliver the latest edition of the South Wales Evening Post, 1942.

High Street, looking up towards the railway station, 1985.

Members of the bowls club at Jersey Park, St Thomas, with trophies won in a successful, mid-1950s season.

Looking down King's Lane on April 16, 2002. The Cardiff Arms public house, later demolished, can be seen on the left at the bottom. The thoroughfare was previously called Morris Lane after the industrialist Morris family of Morriston who once operated a coal wharf near its lower end.

Lovely weather for ducks! Glamorgan Cricket Club captain Hugh Morris and new signing Ottis Gibson sample the weather at St Helen's ground that forced the annual day-night match to be called off on July 13, 1998. Ottis Gibson became the bowling coach of the successful England team that won back the Ashes from Australia in the 2015 Test series.

The 1960s built Unifloc company building, later occupied by Rowecord, prior to demolition, August 27, 2005.

Youngsters enjoy a playground ride alongside the boating lake at Singleton Park, 1969.

Crowds throng the Gower show at Penrice Castle on August 2, 1979.

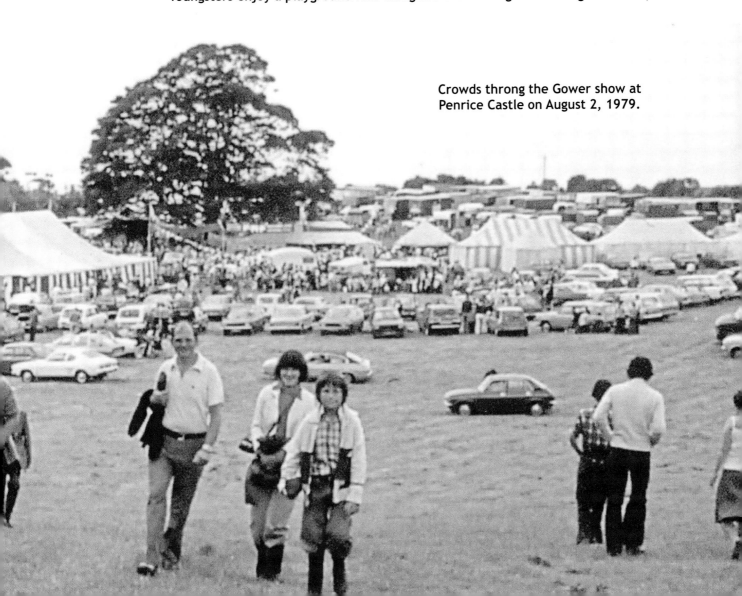

Students of the Upper VI Arts group at Dynevor Comprehensive School, 1978. Among them, on the left of the middle row, is Swansea entertainer and personality Kevin Johns, MBE.

Cefn Hengoed School soccer team, winners of the C Rogers Cup 15 - 1 on aggregate, seen after the second leg of the competition at Caernarvon Town in 1983. The Cefn Hengoed team didn't lose a game in four years.

An aerial view across the city showing Singleton Hospital and part of the university campus, early 1980s.

Some of the spectators in the members enclosure during the Glamorgan v West Indies match at St Helen's Ground, July, 1973. Glamorgan lost by an innings, but batsman Alan Jones scored 90 and 60 for them.

Members of the Baptist Mission Church, Mansel Road, Bonymaen, 1959.

Industrial premises alongside the River Tawe, early 1970s. The BT tower can be seen in the background left, and Weaver's flour mill on the right.

Waun Wen Junior School pupils commemorate World Children's Day, 1965.

Fan-tastic!

The Swans fly high!

Hordes of delighted Swansea City fans throng Glamorgan Street near Vetch Field during the late 1980s. They were joining in a victory parade after one of the successes in the club's long and proud history. INSET: All smiles from the players aboard the open top double decker bus that took the team on its tour of celebration.

Swansea Corporation housing nearing completion at Gomer Road, Townhill, March 1938.

With a city panorama in the background the paddle steamer Waverley turns with the aid of a bow cable before heading out of the River Tawe on a packed cruise, June 1988. INSET: A close-up of some of the passengers aboard the vessel.

The ruins of Morris Castle, off Trewyddfa Road, Landore, 1920s. Sometimes referred to as Castle Graig it was built between 1768 and 1774 by Sir John Morris to house workers at his nearby collieries and copper works.

Looking down Wind
Street, late 1960s.

A group of students from Swansea Art College during an outing in 1967.

Bar staff take time out for a photograph to mark the last night of operation of the Irvine Club, Mumbles, September, 1987.

A South Wales Transport AEC Bridgemaster bus approaches the junction of Delhi Street with St Ledger Crescent as it negotiates its route through St Thomas in the snow, 1965.

A fascinating Marina-side panorama, 2008.

John Jones, owner of Mumbles Dairy, with his first motor vehicle after he changed from horse drawn milk floats, in the 1940s. The dairy was just east of the current seafront car park at the bottom of Newton Road.

Children of employees of the Tom Smith & Clarke chain works, Crymlyn Burrows, during a Christmas party, 1958.

Two young lads enjoy the delights of burying themselves in the sand near The Slip, 1965.

Sunny days

The sands at The Slip have long held

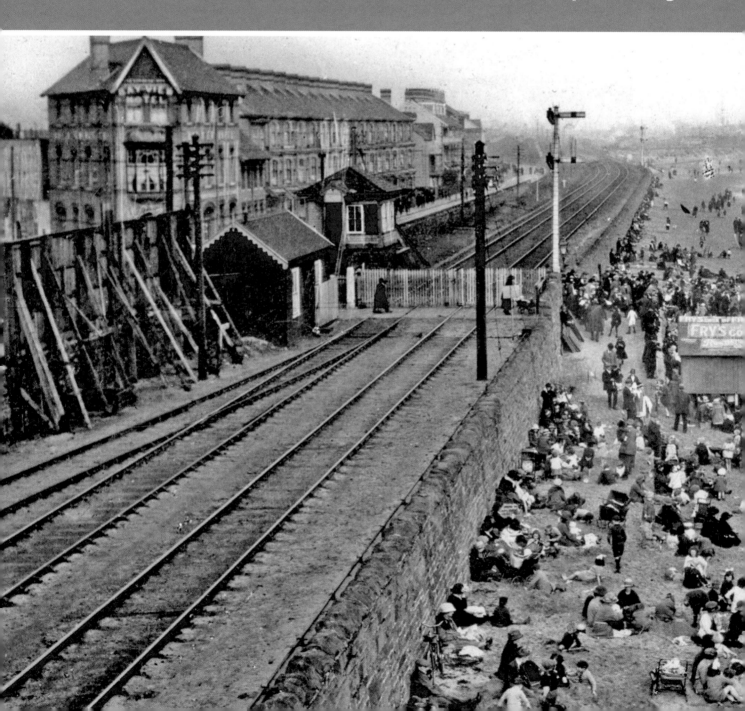

Family fun at The Slip, complete with deck chairs and ice cream, August 1957.

on the sands

an attraction when days out beckoned

As the tide recedes, crowds flock to the sands at The Slip in the early 1900s. Their dress was obviously far different to that seen on sunny days in current times though!

Scores of children enjoyed the entertainment provided by Peter Brough and his loveable character Archie Andrews at Dunvant Park, 1950.

A steam powered Mumbles train with a packed consignment of passengers approaches Southend station on its way to Swansea, 1925. It is seen close to the Knab Rock slipway where Verdi's ice cream parlour is now located.

A tree lined and almost traffic free
Walter Road, in the early 1920s.

Participants in a production of the Merchant of
Venice, at Bishop Gore School, Christmas 1957.

A train on the high level railway line, linking Swansea Docks with the South Dock passes Weaver's grain store, 1955. Sainsbury's car park is here now.

Members of the 36th Swansea (Sketty) Wesley Cub Scout pack with leaders, February 28, 1993.

New houses under construction opposite
the old at Kilvey, mid-1960s.

If you'd looked south east across the River Tawe from
the top of the BT tower, on February 28, 1985, this
would have been the view that greeted you.

With its futuristic design this building, erected among much controversy, was originally the headquarters of West Glamorgan County Council. Seen during construction in 1983, it is currently home to Swansea City Council.

Going up . . .

As one new landmark appeared on the

Coal fired Tir John Power Station, Port Tennant, was built between 1931 and 1935 by Swansea Corporation as part of an unemployment relief scheme. It was the biggest engineering project in Wales at the time and the largest power station in Britain. It operated from 1936 to 1976 and is viewed here from Bonymaen in the 1960s, with BP's storage tank farm at Crymlyn Burrows, behind. Alongside, a memory jerker of demolition day for the power station's three chimneys. With one of the three landmarks gone, the second begins to fall and eventually just one is left. That too, didn't remain upright for long however and its bricks came crashing to the ground shortly after the far right photograph was taken in the 1980s.

and coming down!

skyline so another vanished from sight

A group of pupils with their teacher and headteacher at Brynhyfryd Junior School, 1985.

A group of friends with the conductor and driver of the Mumbles train at Oystermouth in 1959. The line was closed in January of the following year.

The people patiently queuing outside Seabourne's Bakery in Llangyfelach Road, Treboeth, were hoping to replenish their bread supplies after a heavy snowfall in 1982.

A group of Swansea lads enjoy a night out together at the Three Lamps public house, overlooking Castle Gardens, mid-1960s.

A winter homecoming during a snowstorm at Llwyn Derw, Fforestfach, 1941.

Howard Martin, right, the person responsible for founding the stained glass department at Swansea College of Art — now ranked the best in the world — discusses a project with student Roger Hayman over lunch in 1969. A prolific figure in Swansea's cultural past, Howard began his involvement with the department in the 1930s. He also ran Celtic Studios in Prospect Place.

Swansea Training College, Townhill, early 1950s. The allotments below the building will have provided a bumper harvest of fresh produce that year.

Top table guests at an event held at the former Holiday Inn, now the Marriott hotel, on October 11, 1989. It was a celebration to mark 50 years of the RM Douglas construction company.

Workmen digging
up the pavement
in Newton Road,
Mumbles, during
June 1975,
take a break from
their labours.
The once popular
Tiffany's
discotheque, now
the site of the
Castle Arcade, is in
the background.

A group of Swansea council employees, all set for a day trip in the early 1950s. War ravaged St Mary's Church can be seen in the background, with rebuilding work yet to start.

Siemens Bessemer Furnace, Landore, 1976. Part of the Siemens steelworks, it was opened as an experimental facility on the site of the Landore Silver and Spelter Works in 1867-69.

Looking eastwards towards the former United Carbon Black works and the AWCO wire and cable plant, Port Tennant, early 1970s. The railway sidings later became the site of the Fabian Way Park and Ride scheme.

King George VI arriving at the Mond Nickel Works, Clydach, during a visit to boost workers' morale during March, 1944. Crowds thronged the kerbside along the route of the cavalcade of cars accompanying the Royal party hoping to catch a glimpse of the king.

Preparing foundations at the junction of Russell Street and Duke Street, when the South Wales Transport company decided to replace its former head office with a modern building in the 1960s. INSET: Demolition of the former South Wales Transport office building latterly owned by Bevan and Buckland Accountants. February 13, 2015.

Pupils of Form 2:3, at Olchfa Comprehensive School, 1987.

Dylan's Cafe Bar which occupied the Grand Hotel's former Hole In The Wall position, High Street, May 16, 2002.

A boarded up Smelters Arms at the Graig, outside the north gate of Llewellyn's Park. It was later converted into housing.

Gallivan's, the Bridge Street, Greenhill pub that started life as The Dublin, a replacement for the original Dublin Arms that was demolished to make way for road improvements at Dyfatty. It is seen here on April 3, 2002, shortly before it closed. The site is now occupied by a supermarket.

The Gors Inn, Heol Y Gors, Townhill, on July 3, 2002. It closed some years later to make way for a convenience store and fish and chip shop.

Last orders please!

Some of the city's once popular, but now vanished, pubs and bars.

The Garibaldi Inn, Western Street, up for sale on April 10, 2003.

The former Zanzi-Ba premises which stood on the corner of the Kingsway and Christina Street as it appeared on April 4, 2002. The building has now been demolished to make way for a car park.

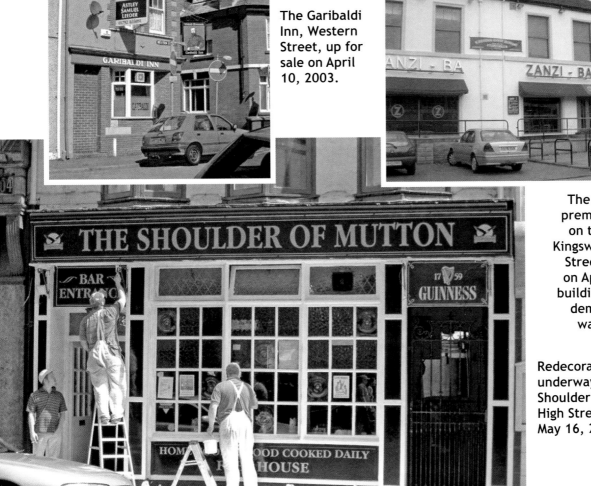

Redecoration underway at The Shoulder of Mutton, High Street, May 16, 2002.

The junction of Fabian Way and Quay Parade near one of the original main entrances to Swansea Docks. Work is underway to remove the railway bridge that crossed two roads here. INSET: Removal of the stonework that supported the bridge across Thomas Street.

Wagons of anthracite from the Dulais Valley snake their way into King's Dock on January 4, 1991, before their cargo is loaded aboard ship for export.

St Thomas Boys School pupils with Mr Jenkins headteacher and Mr Bath, right, their teacher in 1938.

Food preparation staff at Littlewood's High Street store, 1959.

Windmill Terrace, St Thomas, 1973. St Thomas School is on the left.

When I grow up perhaps I'll have one of these! — a young boy sits astride a relative's motorcycle, 1965.

Residents of Upper Killay prepare to embark on an annual outing, 1935.

The spire of St Thomas Church, covered in a web of scaffolding while undergoing repairs, June 1977.

A group of Singleton Park workmen all set for a day out. Their mode of transport would probably have fulfilled a far different task during their weekday labours.

Brothers Shaun, left, and Kevin Tobin join together to win the first Swansea Valley half marathon organised by Swansea Valley Round Table in 1980. The brothers' time was 69 minutes 42 seconds.

Swansea Dock tank locomotive 1152, on '17 Target duty', passes the former Merchant Navy Hotel on the left, as it hauls a train load of imported timber along the low level railway line that ran from Kings Dock to the South Dock where it was bound for the Gregor Bros. timber yard. It is in Victoria Road, October 1959.

In Hawaiian costumes and carnival mood are employees of Microlink Industries, Fforestfach which operated in the former Corgi Toys factory, early 1990s.

Work underway to remove the floodlight stanchions during demolition of the Vetch Field, former home of Swansea City FC. Both views were captured from Glamorgan Terrace, 2012. INSET: a close-up of a workman using a cutting torch to remove part of the structure.

EAST TERRACE | EAST STAND

Britannia class locomotive 70017 'Arrow' at High Street station about to depart
with the Red Dragon express, the 7.30 am Carmarthen to Paddington train, 1957.

Pupils at Cwm Infants school with Miss Powell, left and Mrs Davies, some of
whom are dressed in traditional Welsh costume for St David's Day, 1968.

A horse and cart travels through Gorseinon with the railway signal box on the right and the cinema on the left, 1930.

Two youngsters alongside the floral gardens at Southend, June 1988. They are standing alongside a former wartime mine that for many years was used as a charity collection box.

Pupils and teachers at Craig Y Nos School, Uplands, 1952.

Early construction work on the Knab Rock slipway, Mumbles, August 1983.

Employees in the body shop at the South Wales Transport bus company's Ravenhill depot, 1976.

A class of pupils at St Thomas Girls School, 1939.

Farmworkers engaged in threshing operations at Lunnon, Gower, with the aid of a steam-powered traction engine,1912.

Llangyfelach Road, Treboeth, looking towards the Gospel Hall, late 1940s.

Members of the second year hockey team at Olchfa Comprehensive School with teachers, 1987.

Colleagues gather to celebrate the retirement of Alf Farrow
from the Louis Marx toy company, Fforestfach, mid-1960s.

A South Wales Transport AEC Renown double decker heads along Glanmor
Road, Uplands, on its way to Port Tennant on service 33, 1964.

This drayman was at the wheel of a Ford D Series lorry. It was the first vehicle to carry the new logo when brewers Watney and Truman united their Welsh operations in the mid-1980s.

Bunting spans Newton Road, Mumbles, in readiness for the Ostreme Festival, 1973.

The dedication of the main
gates of St Helen's ground of
Swansea Cricket & Football
Club, situated opposite
The Cricketers public house.

Cefn Coed Hospital,
Cockett, early 1950s.

Langland Corner after a heavy snowfall, February, 1985.

A silhouette of the Mumbles lighthouse provides the backdrop for a demonstration visit by an American type of lifeboat in August 1964.

A group of friends enjoy their New year's Eve celebrations at the Gasworks Club, 1965.

Members of the Women's Junior Air Corps march past Victoria Park on Oystermouth Road while taking part in the Remembrance Day Parade, November 11, 1949. The track of the Mumbles Railway can be seen on the right.

Three young boys who grew up in St Helen's Avenue pose for a photo in Victoria Park, 1951.

Test piling underway for construction of the Liberty Stadium, alongside Neath Road, Landore, 2003.

Rise of a premier

The Liberty Stadium — proud home

The terraces of the Liberty Stadium's North Stand begin to take shape.

The steel framework that was to become the Liberty Stadium, early 2004. In 2015 the structuire celebrated its 10th birthday.

sporting landmark

to Swansea City FC and the Ospreys

Viewed from Neath Road, Landore, this web of steelwork provided an early guide to the shape of the Liberty Stadium.

Dunvant RFC playing Japan's national rugby team, at Broadacre, on November 2, 1993.
Dunvant led at one point in an exciting encounter, but were eventually beaten by the tourists.

The stone laying ceremony of Wesley Memorial Methodist Church, Townhill, Saturday, July 25, 1959.

These cheery women worked at Hodges sewing factory, Fforestfach, early 1950s.

Class J4 at Waun Wen Junior School, with teacher Mr Griffiths, 1966.

This 1980s view shows Landore viaduct scything across the embryonic
Swansea Enterprise Park, with much cleared land behind.

Bridging the gap

Landore railway viaduct remains one of Swansea's most important transport arteries. It dates as far back as 1850. Originally, it was a 1,847 ft long structure designed by Isambard Kingdom Brunel which was constructed in timber. The structure was updated in 1889, using wrought-iron for the central span. Between 1978 and 1979, the rest of the viaduct was re-decked with steel beams. It's life has spanned many decades and the images here depict it during some of these.

Cadbury Castle hauls the 10.30am Swansea to Paddington express across Landore viaduct on its journey to London on February 4, 1959.

Landore viaduct acts like a picture frame for this snowy view across the Lower Swansea Valley, in 1982.

Mumbles Pier undergoing refurbishment during 1987. The former lifeboat house can be seen in the background.

Members young and old of the congregation of Eaton Road Methodist Church, Brynhyfryd, all set for a Whitsun outing, early 1960s.

Members of Singleton Hospital's drama group during rehearsals for the pantomime Alice in Wonderland which they staged in the mid-1980s.

The Pottery Bridge that once carried a railway line across the north end of the North Dock. With the dock filled in it was no longer needed by the time this picture was taken in 1965. The upper Strand and High Street railway station are behind.

Players and officials of Cwm Albion football team, late 1940s.

Members of Wesley Memorial Methodist Church, Townhill, seated in the street outside, before the official opening of the new building on Saturday, June 25, 1960.

The BP oil company's tank storage farm at Crymlyn Burrows, early 1960s. The site, alongside the Fabian Way dual carriageway, is now home to a new complex of Swansea University buildings.

Swansea Docks viewed from Lewis Street, St Thomas, early 1960s.

Players and officials of the Birchgrove AFC team which played
in the Pic-Up Spares Swansea Sunday League, 1994.

Prime Minister Ted Heath arrives by helicopter for a visit to
the Morganite Electrical factory, Morriston, 1973.

An impressive line-up of lorries at the North Dock depot of British Road Services, alongside The
Strand, 1960. The rear of commercial properties in High Street can be seen in the background.

Looking eastwards across the Quay Parade bridge over the River Tawe and St Thomas, from the top of the city's BT tower on February 28, 1985. The scene has changed significantly during the intervening years.

A sad end for a proud locomotive. Royal Scot class locomotive, The Manchester Regiment, reaches the end of the line at Bird's scrapyard, Morriston, March 1965.

Gorseinon versus Loughor inter-club karate tournament competitors, March 2008.

Members of St Paul's Church Sunday School, Sketty, 1950 . . . complete with an obliging canine friend!

The Meridian Tower rises skywards on March 30, 2008. It became Wales' tallest residential building.

South Wales Transport bus company signwriter Gareth Davies with coachbuilders at Ravenhill, alongside one of the company's early Regent V double deckers, mid-1960s. A sister vehicle, MCY 407, is now preserved at Swansea Bus Museum.

Children of employees of the Louis Marx toy factory, Fforestfach, enjoying a Christmas party, 1955.

SWANSEA TOWN A.F.C LTD.

A group of Swansea Town players from the early 1950s all set for a training session at Vetch Field.

Swansea City player Mark Harris scoring a second goal during the club's game against Exeter, at the Vetch, 1994.

Vetch Field groundsman Dave Hanley prepares the ground for the upcoming season on June 23, 1997, with an assistant in the background.

Swans snapshots

Halcyon days at Vetch Field — the old home of Swansea City!

Swansea City hero, legend and first team coach, Alan Curtis in action as a player, May 19, 1986.

Looking down on Swansea University campus from the north east with the coastline in the background, mid-1970s. Singleton Hospital can also be seen on the right.

Cranes involved in the
construction of the replacement
New Cut road bridge over the
River Tawe, 1963.

Contractors lay paving stones at the junction of lower Union Street and Nelson Street,
between the Quadrant Centre entrance and the Thomas Thomas warehouse, mid-1980s.

Sidney Clarke advertised himself as being the largest decorating supplier in South Wales in 1903. His shop was at 28 Waterloo Street.

Principal guests at the wedding of Doreen and Bert Prosser, at St Thomas Community Centre, on Saturday, July 9, 1949. In later times the building was demolished and replaced by housing.

Wedding ways

Mount Pleasant Baptist Church, Kingsway, was the scene of this wedding between Barrie Pember and Jennifer Punter, on March 7, 1964. The couple celebrated their Golden Wedding in 2014.

The wedding of Doris Edwards to
William Matthews which took place at
Llangyfelach Church on February 14, 1942.

A beautiful bride and a beautiful bouquet — not
forgetting the proud groom with his gloves in hand!

Children play alongside the graveyard of St Matthew's Church, High Street, 1920.

A horse-drawn Cambrian United Dairies milk cart at Mumbles, early 1950s.

Members of the Jeffreys family with their horse and trap about
to set off to gather cockles on the marsh at Llanmorlais, 1956.

A party of charabanc trippers arrives at Stephens' Tea
Room alongside the Post Office at Oxwich, early 1920s.

A group of council
workers repair a
vandalised bus
shelter at
Mumbles Road,
during the
mid-1980s.

Meredith Kneath and Sam Jeffreys with
two prize-winning cattle exhibits at the
Gower Show, mid-1950s.

Looking across Castle Gardens, into Castle Street, during the early 1950s
when the attractive and popular location was still in its infancy.

They came from every part of the surrounding community, more than 200 of them, young and
old to sample the treats at a bumper Christmas party organised by members of the Wesley
Memorial Methodist Church, Townhill, in the Church hall on Tuesday, December 6, 1966.

Except for
access

A summertime view through the trees
from Mumbles towards Newton, 1975.

This group of schoolchildren were pupils at one of Swansea's private schools during the early 1950s.

A shopper admires some of the tempting greengrocery on offer at this shop in Newton Road, Mumbles, June 1975.

Participants in a Christian Procession of Witness which wound its way from St Mary's Church in the city centre, up to the summit of Kilvey Hill, one Good Friday during the mid-1970s. INSET: The wooden cross which some of the participants carried at the head of the procession.

A group of South Wales Transport engineering staff alongside a newly delivered AEC recovery vehicle, 1979.

The maintenance shop at Teddington Components, Woodville Road, Pontarddulais, mid-1970s.

Loading aluminium slabs onto a lorry at the North Dock depot of British Road Services, 1960.

A sad farewell — the initials of the Unit Superheater Engineering company are all that remain on the gates of the premises after it awaits demolition following closure.

A gathering of children and parents outside the health clinic that was held at the old black hut, Fairwood, in the late 1940s.

Bonymaen Rugby Club members celebrate promotion to Division Two of the West Wales League, April 30, 1994.

Construction work underway on the new road bridge over the River Loughour, late 1980s.

Waun Wen Junior School football team with teachers and headmaster Mr AC Allen on the left, 1965-66.

The former Mumbles Railway tramcar shed at Rutland Street mid-1970s, shortly before it was demolished as part of a redevelopment scheme.

Reconstruction of the roadway system around Kingsway roundabout, 2007.

The railway track at Swansea Bay station almost covered by wind-blown sand, on June 4, 1965.

A decaying corner shop on Llangyfelach Road, Brynhyfryd in the mid-1960s.

The Quadrant Centre
bus station, 1992.

A group of friends from St Helen's Avenue Boys in Victoria Park, early 1960s.

The monitoring station at the upper Lliw reservoir, 2009.

There were 21 candles on the cake to celebrate the coming of age of the Sisterhood of Wesley Memorial Methodist Church, Townhill, in May 1960. Mrs E Nott of nearby Gwynedd Gardens, was chosen to blow them out as she had been a member of the Sisterhood since its inception. Her efforts are watched by the Minister, Rev H Facer and fellow members.

The dry ski slope at Morfa covered in a liberal dose of the real thing, 2003. Sadly, it had closed by this time.

An icy view of Pluck Lake in Morfa, 2003.

Snow covered and almost impassable, Rhyd y Defaid Drive, Sketty, with an abandoned car, February 2009. In the distance another motorist carries out a slip, sliding manoeuvre.

A frozen Singleton Park lake and snow covered playground, February 2009.

The clubhouse at Swansea Cricket and Football Club, St Helens, 2008.

Looking along the shoreline at Southend, Mumbles, on a gloomy day in 2006.

A close-up of the unique glass frontage of the Carlton Cinema, Oxford Street, in the 1980s. The building has been home to the city's Waterstones book store for 20 years this year.

The signalman opens the gates to allow pedestrians to cross at The Slip after the passage of an incoming train, 1910. This was before construction of the Slip Bridge.

With the Botanical Gardens at Singleton Park in full bloom, the cherubs on the fountain had plenty to look at, late summer, 2007.

A quiet afternoon at Pontardulais railway station, 1957.

Participants in an event at Waterstones bookshop in Oxford Street to publicise the newly released film Twin Town in 1997 which was set in and around Swansea. They include, from the left: the film's co-writer Paul Durden, Rhys Ifans who played the lead character, Jeremy Lewis and front right, Kevin Allen, co-writer and director.

The Slip bridge, Mumbles Road, in 1999 and right, despite the efforts of campaigners, shortly before its removal in 2003. It had been opened in October 1915 to allow pedestrians to cross from Victoria Park onto Swansea Sands at The Slip without facing the danger of crossing the railway lines there.

Slipping away

The bridge is placed in the recreation ground after removal from its site on February 28, 2004.

Heavy duty, lorry mounted cranes remove the 130 tonne structure during the early morning of Sunday, February 28, 2004.

From the beach looking up to the stone remains of the abutments, barricaded by scaffolding and safety fencing, 2006.

A site inspection during the public inquiry into the right of way and future replacement of the Slip bridge with inquiry inspector Mrs Sue Arnott leading the way, June, 2010.

A tram heads back down Eaton Road near its junction with Llangyfelach Road at Pentre Estyll, on its way into the town centre in the early 1900s. The Commercial Inn dominated the junction and no doubt was a popular local hostelry.

Looking across Swansea Bay over Mumbles pier and the now replaced RNLI lifeboat house, 1972.

The pilot cutter Seamark, after being deliberately grounded on Swansea beach, for cleaning of its hull, 1971.

A class of pupils with their teacher at St Thomas School, 1967.

Railway arches alongside what is now Fabian Way, near the SA1 development, 1968.
They stood between the railway bridge and the main docks entrance, opposite Thomas Street.

The Press Hall at the South Wales Evening Post, shortly after the
newspaper moved into its new Adelaide Street offices, 1968.

Recovering the Porteynon Lifeboat after a practice, early 1900s. The lifeboat was launched on a carriage
pulled by six horses. The carriage wheels had steel plates on them to prevent it sinking into the sand.

Looking up the River Tawe towards the Liberty Stadium, home of Swansea City FC and The Ospreys rugby team, 2008.

The Taliesin theatre, left, remains the same, but the Swansea University building on the right has undergone a refurbishment project and become the campus reception centre.

Pupils of class J4A at St Helen's School, together with their teacher and headteacher, 1970.

Younger members of Wesley Memorial Methodist Church, Townhill,
at a Christmas party held in the church hall, 1958.

Construction work nears completion on the original Swansea Leisure Centre,
1976. The building was opened by HRH Queen Elizabeth II the following year.

Looking along Mumbles Road, past the former grandstand at Swansea Cricket and Football Club, late 1970s.

Passengers queue for an approaching tram, perhaps to convey them into the centre of Swansea, as a typical daily scene unfolds at Uplands Crescent, home to a string of independent retailers, more than a century ago in 1910.

Oystermouth Road, with the former Mumbles Railway tram depot in Rutland Street on the left, late 1960s.

Timely changes

The four images here show the many faces of time as portrayed by the intricate patterns of the floral clocks that have been cleverly crafted by Swansea Council's gardeners down the decades. The respective dates are, from the top left, and — clockwise of course — 1913, 1975, 1918 and 1913.

The chassis cleaning bay at the South Wales Transport Company's main depot at Ravenhill, late 1950s.

The Promenade, Southend, Mumbles, 1905.

Langland Bay was a scene of destruction and devastation after severe storms and heavy seas reduced beach huts and tent bases to matchwood during October 1967.

Members of the Sergeants' Mess with their wives and partners at the Drill Hall, Richardson Street, 1962.

All Saint's Church, Kilvey Road, Kilvey, 1972.

It was a tight squeeze as the Liverpool registered tug, Crosby,
eased the MV World Reliance into the Kings Dock lock, 1971.

Crowds look skyward at Fairwood Airport during an air display, in the 1970s.

Staff of South Wales Transport's engineering section at a
retirement function for one of their colleagues, early 1960s.

Almost traffic free, this was Sketty Cross in 1939.

Fortes Ice cream parlour, and flats at Limeslade, 1980.

Gendros Garage, Fforestfach early 1980s with some typical vehicles of the period alongside.

The lake in Brynmill Park, April 1966, a haven of peace and tranquility that in its heyday attracted people from not just the locality, but miles around.

Swansea University's student village, Hendrefoilan, near Killay, during its construction in 1992. It was sold in 2013 to help fund the new science and innovation campus on Fabian Way and is destined to be demolished to make way for a development of 270 new homes.

Two redundant submarines, S153, Sea Scout and S89 Seraph, which had been used in a wartime deception mission, retold in the film The Man Who Never Was, at Swansea Docks shortly before being towed to shipbreakers Thos Ward at Giant's Grave on the River Neath, in the mid-1960s.

Looking across the Maritime Quarter towards the South Dock
basin, before the construction of housing, October 17, 2004.

The pavilion at a snow-covered Ravenhill Park, winter 1947.

The Grand temperance, family and commercial hotel, on the corner of High Street and Alexandra Road, opposite High Street railway station, 1903. It later became the Great Western Hotel. The current Grand Hotel which stands on the opposite corner, shared by Ivey Place and High Street, was not built until 1932.

A South Wales Transport AEC Regent V double decker heading along a busy Oxford Street, past the market entrance, 1976.

This family butchers shop at 89, Neath Road, Hafod, with a row of pigs hanging outside was an importer of American and Colonial meats according to the sign above the window in 1911.

Looking eastwards along Oystermouth Road, towards the Slip bridge
after the removal of the Mumbles Railway track, March, 1968.

This picture, taken following the wedding of Orinda Lewis and David John Williams in
1933 includes the 10 girls and one boy who at the time comprised the Williams family.

The midday Shrewsbury to Swansea Victoria train hauled by Black Five locomotive 45406, passes Dunvant signal box, May 14, 1964.

Swansea docks tank locomotive 1152 running light past Weaver's flour mill, Quay Parade, October 24, 1959.

A mixed goods train passes through Llanmorlais railway station, Gower, 1956.

A Shrewsbury to Swansea Victoria train at Pontardulais railway station, 1963.

A class at Parklands Infants School, with their teacher, 1980.

The Exchange public house, later the Kon-Tiki, on the corner of Green Dragon Lane and The Strand, 2003.

Looking down from The Slip bridge onto an Oystermouth Road undergoing significant roadworks after the closure of the Mumbles Railway and the line to Swansea Victoria station, mid-1970s.

Swansea West MP Alan Williams opens a fete organised by residents and staff of Hanover Court, Tycoch Road, August 14, 1990. He had previously opened the care complex in November 1977. He is seen being thanked by Maggie Guard, warden, her husband Cliff and Lindsey Thomas, right, management representative.

A fascinating rooftop view looking across to the gasworks site now occupied by Tesco's Marina store, taken from the top of the BT Tower in the Strand, 1973. In the distance, the South Dock, Gregor Bros. timber yard and homes in the Paxton Street area are visible.

The Community Centre, Cefn Road, Bonymaen, with Tir
John Power Station in the background, early 1970s.

Mirador Crescent, Uplands, early 1900s.

The Tivoli Fruit Shop,
run by proprietor
CJ Jones at the Tivoli
Buildings, Mumbles,
early 1950s.

A group of friends at
Grenfell Park Road,
St Thomas, 1944.

Looking down on a now, much changed part of Swansea, bordered by railway lines, the River Tawe and the South Dock, mid-1920s.

Fun and frolics on one of the floats that formed part of the Dunvant carnival parade, 1982.

The eastbound approach to New Cut bridge, 1973.

This entry in the 1981 Swansea Carnival had very much a Second World War American influence with its Jeep and nurses.

A group of Loughor senior citizens on a day out, 1962.

A group of friends take a break on a wall alongside Gower Road, Upper Killay, early 1950s.

Committee members of Swansea Cricket and Football Club, during a presentation ceremony, 1964.

Shoppers throng Oxford Street, 1985.

Pupils from Manselton Junior School, outside the Brangwyn Hall, during Swansea's Youth Proms, 1991.

Dunvant Rugby Club players celebrate their success at remaining
in Division One of the Heineken League, April 30, 1994.

One of the impressive floats which took part in Bishopston Carnival, 1976.

The Bay View Hotel stands proudly at the junction of St Helen's Road and Oystermouth Road, mid-1930s. The tram was waiting to return to High Street railway station.

Mansel Road, Bonymaen, mid-1970s.

Approaching the junction of Mumbles Road and The Mayals, Blackpill, June, 1975.

Panda cars and police officers during an incident at Delhi Street, St Thomas, 1972.

Demolition day nears for the Station Inn, Sebastopol Street, St Thomas, 1969.

The derelict Weaver's building towers over Quay Parade 1976. For many years it was considered by many as an ugly eyesore on one of Swansea's main traffic gateways.

Weaver's flour mill shortly before the start of its demolition.

Concrete colossus

Weaver's flour mill stood as a major landmark in Swansea for nearly 100 years. It was the first entirely reinforced concrete building to be erected in Britain and designed by the French engineer Francois Hennebique, who developed this system of reinforcement. His main patent for the Hennebique system dates from 1897, the year the mill was constructed. The mill was built on a site beside the basin of the former North Dock. It was six storeys high, with its lower floor cantilevered around three metres over loading bays. Unusually perhaps, it was constructed using cement, aggregate and steel imported from France. The building survived wartime bombing, but was demolished and the site eventually utilised as the car park of Sainsbury's supermarket. The North Dock basin was filled in the 1960s. All that remains today is a segment of the structure which can be seen alongside the riverside pathway just outside the car park.

A civic thumbs up as Swansea's Mayor starts the demolition of Weaver's flour mill in 1984, a job far more difficult than contractors Coslett had bargained for.

A tangled mass of twisted metal and rubble during demolition of the Weaver's building.

Members of Garden Village Football Club, Gorseinon, who obviously had good reason to pop the champagne corks.

Dunvant RFC who were celebrating champagne style after becoming Heineken League Division Two champions in 1993.

The David Evans department store in Princess Way shortly before demolition, 2008.

A group of Fforestfach Scouts enjoy some hi-jinks.

Originally the home of the South Wales Evening Post, this building opened in 1968. It was stripped of its former identity when the newspaper relocated to offices in the Urban Village, High Street.

Swansea promenade, June 4, 1965. Still separating it from the beach is the defunct and almost sand covered track of the Swansea Victoria to Shrewsbury railway line.

Members of St Joseph's Under 11 football squad with an array of trophies during the club's presentation evening, 1984.

A Leyland National bus on route 12 crawls up the steep incline to Terrace Road before tackling the even steeper section to Graiglwyd Square, Townhill, 1975.

Pupils of Pentrehafod School with members of the National Theatre Company who conducted a workshop and performance of the production Measure for Measure at the school on March 1, 2002.

Participants in a Gower ploughing match held at
Parc le Breos, Penmaen, January 27, 1959.

The newly opened LC2 leisure centre occupies centre stage in this 2008 maritime panorama.

A South Wales Transport double decker on service 77 from Morriston to Limeslade, passes the offices of the South Wales Evening Post and Herald of Wales newspapers in Castle Bailey Street, 1962.

There was plenty to see and do at Craig Y Nos School's summer fete, 2000.

The Morris family who lived in this prefab at No 2 site,
Fairwood Common after the war, pose for the camera in 1964.

D. Jones & Company
operated this clothing
store at Nos. 2 & 3 High
Street, 1903.

A family enjoy a welcome rest outside the Post Office at Rhossili, July 24, 1984.

Five lads proudly display medals earned after success in a swimming competition, early 1960s.

Trawlers at Swansea fish market, Prince of Wales Dock. Tied
up in the foreground is the restored steam tug, Thomas, 1979.

Three council
workers with a
lorry at Townhill,
1960s.

Bryn Edwards, a builder, based in Upper Killay, alongside his lorry, 1959.

Looking up Princess Way towards the Kingsway, mid-1950s with Castle Gardens in full bloom and people relaxing on the benches.

Oystermouth Girls' School gym class, 1947.

Traffic at
Fforestfach Cross,
early 1980s.

A group of children with their gifts from Santa at a Christmas party at the Northgate sewing factory, Fforestfach, 1968.

Members of the Irvine Club, Mumbles, who took part in, and won, a fancy dress competition at Barton Hall, July 1978.

Members of the Embassy Club in front of its entrance gates, 1952.

Rugby player Richard Webster in action with the All Whites, March 1992.

A City Mini bus waits alongside the bus station
at Oystermouth Square, June, 1988.

177

Employees of the Mettoy toy factory, Fforestfach and their families during a trip to Blackpool, 1951.

The darts team at the Cardiff Arms public house, The Strand, mid-1980s.

A group of lorry drivers employed at the British Road Services, North Dock depot, early 1960s.

Looking from Castle Square along Castle Bailey Street towards Castle Street, 1904.

Residents of Linden Avenue, West Cross, celebrating the wedding of Prince Charles and Lady Diana, 1981.

Landore Wesleyan Methodist
Chapel, Wern Road, 1960.

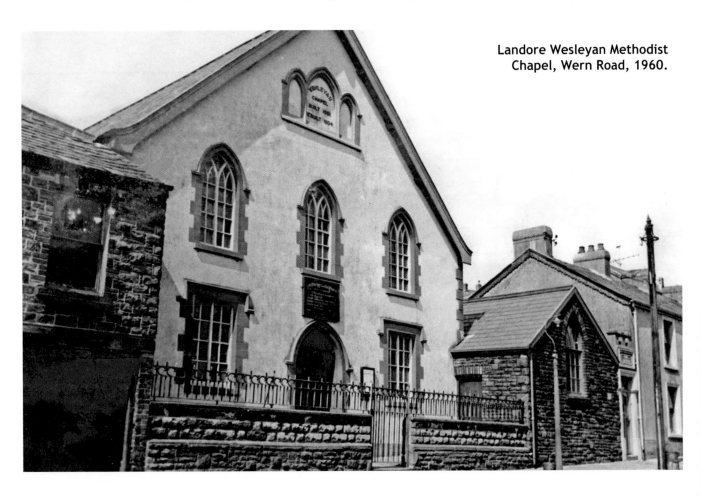

The entrance to Cwmfelin tinplate works, Llangyfelach Road, mid-1960s.

Constables from Swansea West police headquarters at Cockett, preparing to board an aircraft at
Fairwood airport in 1981 to take part in a charity fundraising parachute jump.
They are, from the left: Phil Jenkins, Phil Burton, Bryndon Evans and Bryan Jenkins.

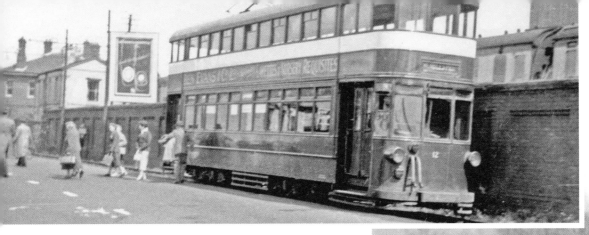

Passengers leave the train at the Rutland Street terminus, mid-1950s.

Rocking rolling & riding

Approaching Oystermouth during the late 1950s. The Tivoli cinema building can just be seen through the trees on the right.

. . . that's how travellers on the Mumbles Train described the experience of riding its route around the glorious sweep of Swansea Bay. Sadly the world's first passenger carrying railway reached its final destination on January 5, 1960. It might have gone, but constantly features in nostalgic conversations far and wide. The scenes here will revive the memory for some and provide clues for those who never knew it, as to why it is such a legend in the city's transport history.

Boarding for Mumbles at the Rutland Street terminus, mid-1950s.

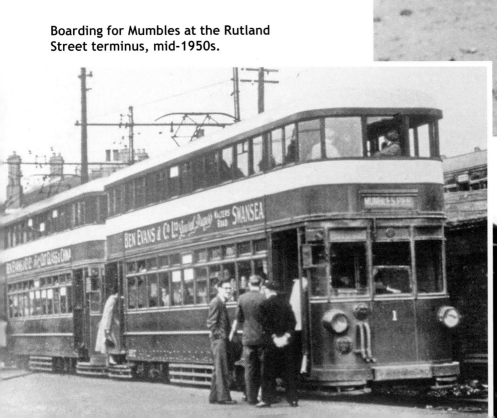

The last regular service train — the 9.55am from Rutland Street for Oystermouth — at St Helen's Station, the Slip.

Opposite the Rutland Street terminus, 1955.

Crowds at Bracelet Bay car park watch the Royal Yacht Britannia passing Mumbles lighthouse, August 1969.

Crazy Mac's discount warehouse took over the former
Texas Homecare store at Fforestfach, February 16, 2002.
The site was later occupied by the Dunelm company.

Members of the 1st Mumbles Scout troop, with their leader, 1914.

Clearing the remains of the burned-down Cardiff Arms public house on August 23, 2003.

Pupils of St Thomas Girls' School, 1938.

A Swansea family enjoy a pony and trap ride during holiday time.

Members of Mumbles Concert Party during a performance at the village's British Legion Club, 1936.

A VE Day party at Norton Road, Mumbles, 1945.

Vehicles wait to pull out of
Alexandra Road and into
High Street, 1983.

A view across the rooftops of Port Tennant, towards Swansea Docks, mid-1960s.

Princess Diana with Lord Lieutenant of Glamorgan, Col. Sir Cenydd Treharne, during a visit to Cefn Hengoed School.

A train to Carmarthen passes over Landore loop, on its way westwards, January 9, 1960.

Steam power reigns in this atmospheric railway scene captured at High Street station on August 21, 1956 as the Red Dragon leaves on its journey to Paddington.